Legacy Moments

Each moment with you is a masterpiece of
Our Legacy

Legacy Moments
by Andrea Boweya

Printed in the United States of America

ISBN 9781622303243

www.xulonpress.com

Table of Contents

This Legacy Moments Belongs To vii

Legacy Moments Introduction...9

A Prayer For You..11

Rethinking Legacy 12

Legacy Moments Defined 15

Legacy Now and in the Future 17

The Power of Your Words 19

Legacy Moments - Your Legacy... 23

About You: Meaningful details, stories and affirming moments with you 25

Transferring love, identity and connection

A Family Legacy: Wisdom and Principles...36

Bridging generational gaps through parental life stories and

the unique legacy in this for you and generations to come

A Priceless Principle 49

Values 51
Defining the core standard of our family or life together

Symbols, Pictures, Art and Visual Representations 58
Symbolic meaning

Life Instructions 69
Important life instructions as a roadmap for the future

Legacy Declarations..81
Decrees and prophetic blessings about your unique purpose

Creating Your Own Legacy Moments Title Pages.....................................90
Unique Pages of Our Legacy

This Legacy Moments belongs to:

_____

Prepared by:

_____

The reasons Legacy Moments was given to you:

You are a heritage from the LORD. Psalm 127:3

Legacy Moments

Introduction

"A good man leaves an inheritance for his children's children…" Proverbs 13:22

Live every moment meaningfully.
Experience every moment intentionally.
Share every day with honour
and record a godly legacy,
one moment at a time.

Meaningful moments will always surpass material gains
Proverbs 8:10-11; Mark 8:36

"O LORD, You are the portion of my inheritance and my cup; You maintain my lot. The lines have fallen to me in pleasant places; Yes, I have a good inheritance." Psalms 16:5-6

A Prayer For You

May you be an invaluable voice for generations to come. May a legacy of godly love, values, declarations, symbolic meaning, and instructions indeed be revealed through you.

May every word penned by you give lasting life to each Legacy Moment. May you be a catalyst to diminish generational failures as you reconnect to your generational strengths.

May every declaration you make truly go beyond the limits of time to transfer exceptional realities for generations to come (Joshua 8:33-35). Ultimately, may you know the rich blessings of God as the foundation of your legacy.

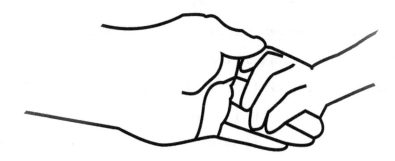

"That the God of our Lord Jesus Christ, the Father of glory, may give to you the spirit of wisdom and revelation in the knowledge of Him, the eyes of your understanding being enlightened; that you may know what is the hope of His calling, what are the riches of the glory of His inheritance in the saints, and what is the exceeding greatness of His power toward us who believe, according to the working of His mighty power." Ephesians 1:17-19

Rethinking Legacy

Oftentimes, when we think of *legacy,* we may think of passing on material wealth (something of worth) to our loved ones at the end of our lives. With the busyness of time, we however tend to forget the importance of passing on the intangible core of life that truly carries the deep value of legacy. While material wealth is important, the essence of legacy is meant to be an intentional transfer of holistic blessings that are passed on from one generation to another, not so much at the end or our lives but throughout our entire life cycle.

When legacy is primarily focused on material wealth that is void of intangible meaning, an essential intergenerational lifeline is broken. Children and loved ones may be left with material possessions; however, without the intangible, yet priceless gift of legacy, they often lose their way in the face of destructive influences, lack of identity, abuse, and other challenging life obstacles. Life becomes like a boat in the wind without an anchor.

For more than a decade, I have served as a counsellor, psychotherapist and family clinician. I am also a mother. From these and many other roles, I have grown to understand the deep importance of legacy and its impact on individual, family, and generational wellbeing. I have been increasingly moved by the demonstrated need in all of us to belong and identify with something bigger than ourselves (a family, a community, a legacy). Whenever this crucial aspect of life is missing, the heart of who we are is in fact profoundly affected. A displaced child/individual innately looks to meet this need and will accept invitation to any alternative, whether good or bad. This need for belonging and identity is that compelling!

Over the years, I have walked with many individuals who have courageously shared their experiences of pain in this search; a pain that is often attached to the hardship of injured or disconnected generational relationships in their lives. In our process of discovery, it is frequently evident that a meaningful legacy is missing or deficient. Similar to the Israelites who suffered through the pain of exile and abuse while the legacy promise of God was available for them, today many individuals and families also live with great potential, but genuinely struggle to purposefully reach forward because they have been disconnected from their divine gifts and identity or the 'who I am' factor.

Through counselling, I have sought to journey with individuals and families into paths of new beginnings. It has been a type of journey that I imagine Jabez may have lived through (1 Chronicles 4:9-10). A journey that is marked by significant difficulties and pain; yet one that is fuelled with a mustered ability to ask for the non-material or intangible gifts that ultimately carry us far beyond the obstacles of life into extraordinary generational possibilities. Like Jabez, this new beginning can become possible for you at any point in life through the knowledge of your own divine generational blessings and legacy.

Legacy is indeed an essential generational gift. It is a gift of blessings, values, prophecies, meaningful stories, life principles, and instructions. Legacy is intergenerational; it carries the wisdom of past generations, while speaking to and with generations to come. A great legacy does not happen by chance; it is rather built on intentional participation and recorded moments. At its root, legacy is ultimately shaped from God's Word to us and our active participation in creatively transferring this gift to every generation.

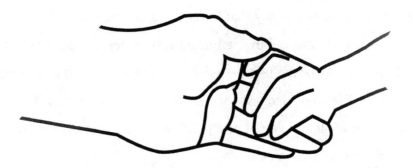

"Then the Lord answered and said: write the vision and make it plain on tablets, that he may run who reads it. For the vision is yet for an appointed time; but at the end it will speak, and it will not lie. Though it tarries, wait for it; because it will surely come, it will not tarry." Habakkuk 2:2-3

Legacy Moments Defined

As your gift of legacy, *Legacy Moments* is your intentional transfer of generational blessings, values, prophecies, meaningful stories, life principles, and instructions to a child or loved one in your life.

Legacy Moments is a creative and participatory guide to rethinking your own legacy. With the turn of every page, *Legacy Moments* will challenge you to consciously stir the deep wealth within yourself, as well as guide you to record and share one of the most valuable gifts you will give to your children or loved ones. One step at a time, *Legacy Moments* will support you to intentionally seek out and participate in everyday legacy building moments. These moments may sometimes seem ordinary or even difficult in experience. Yet they also have the potential to be powerful in meaning as we pay close attention to them. *Legacy Moments* will also allow you to bridge generational gaps by supporting you to record legacy which intentionally include unique wisdom from your own life story and that of past generations. *Legacy Moments* is then purposefully shared with your child or loved one at a meaningful time that best fits their need to be empowered toward full purpose and destiny.

Legacy Moments will help you to:

- Transfer love, identity and connection through meaningful details, affirming moments and stories about your child or loved one.

- Bridge generational gaps by sharing your own story and the unique legacy that you are to your child, loved ones, and generations to come.
- Share values that define the core standard of your family and life together.
- Communicate invaluable messages and defining meaning through symbols, pictures, art, and visual representations.
- Share important life instructions as a roadmap for the future.
- Make declarations and prophetic blessings, with the use of Scripture, about your child or loved one's unique gifts and purpose both now and in the future.
- Create your own Legacy Moments title pages which would allow you to share unique elements of your legacy

"Therefore know that the LORD your God, He is God, the faithful God who keeps covenant and mercy for a thousand generations with those who love Him and keep His commandments;"

Deuteronomy 7:9 (NIV)

Legacy Now and in the Future

The following are two biblical examples of recorded legacy and how legacy worked to radically transform generations both in the present and in the future.

Legacy in the present

In Exodus 17:14, after the Israelites gained victory over the Amalekites, the Lord instructed Moses to record and share a legacy of success with Joshua. Joshua represented the next generation who lived and served in and after Moses' time. "Then the LORD said to Moses, "Write this on a scroll as something to be remembered and make sure that Joshua hears it, because I will completely blot out the name of Amalek from under heaven." (Exodus 17:14 NIV). In fact, what was recorded on this scroll was the heart of a great promise! It signified that the former pattern of disobedience and failure in war, once known to generations before Joshua, was now completely removed from the reality of his generation. This became an amazing foundation to Joshua's generational legacy of success.

Based on God's word and the practical experience of winning this war, Moses' legacy to Joshua reinforced the fact that success in life comes not on the sole merit of human strength but through our reliance on the power of God (Exodus 17:8-13; Proverbs 3:5). Joshua's generation not only received this legacy, but also believed and lived by it as their true inheritance. As a result, this generation was marked by unshakable victory and success. Even when faced with tremendous odds, they consistently overcame through the generational principle of obedience, boldness and reliance on the strength of God as their legacy.

Legacy in the future

In 1 Chronicles 4:9-10, Jabez is highlighted as an honourable man in the midst of his extended family tree. In fact, the honour of Jabez's story is intricately tied to a compelling blessing that was given to his generational tribe many years before his time (Genesis 49:8-10 & Deuteronomy 33:7). Between the initial time of this blessing and Jabez's life, the Israelites had lived through extensive years of exile, disconnection, and pain. It is even noted in 1 Chronicles 4:9 that Jabez was named according to this painful experience. Yet, in a profound moment of reconnection to the power of his generational legacy, Jabez defied the odds in his day. He in fact activated his inheritance by declaring what was prophesied and written about him many generations before his time. You see, it did not matter so much that time had passed. What truly mattered was that in spite of Jabez's circumstances then, there was an existing declaration of his identity for him to hold on to. By accessing this legacy, he was rightly reminded of who he was and in turn made this his only truth. As a result, Jabez's reality was then a life of blessings and ultimate deliverance from the pain, sorrow, and strains of exile in his past. Like Jabez, you too have a rich legacy history with a destiny to extend this legacy into your future.

"This is what the LORD, the God of Israel, says: Write in a book all the words I нave spoken to you." Jeremiah 30:2 (NIV)

The Power of Your Words

When your words are written from the heart and genuinely guided by the purposes of God, they will have lasting impact. In fact, by the wisdom of God, what may seem like simple words now will become a lasting legacy through these pages. Throughout the Bible, we see that the faithfulness of God always stirred connection between His word and the present generation through ongoing meaningful moments. Everyday of your life, this same connection could be forged through you. The truth is, you have something special to offer in the generational legacy of God. You are an important link in sharing and carrying on the unique legacy of your family.

The Bible remains the greatest example of generational legacy through words. Whether as the direct voice of God, His voice through someone else, or an actual account of experiences, the Bible embodies a clear investment in transferring a godly legacy to every generation through the Word of God. Written in a specific time for a specific generation, this same word is yet deeply impactful for us today.

Biblical example of the generational power of legacy through recorded words

Israel (Jacob) and his children are described as a chosen people who in fact were given the blessing of previous generations. The blessing of fruitfulness and increase given to Adam in Genesis 1:28 is reflected in the blessing given to Abraham in Genesis 12:2-3 and 13:14-17. A continuation of this legacy was then declared to Isaac even before he was born. The Lord said, "I will establish My covenant with him [Isaac] for an everlasting covenant, and with his descendants after him" (Genesis 17:19b). Isaac then becomes the father of Jacob and so the blessing is passed on generationally down through the ultimate lineage of Jesus Christ, who is the embodiment of the Word Himself (John 1:14).

The words of legacy through setbacks, stumbling blocks, or disconnection

In Exodus 1, the Bible describes the reality of the Israelites in Egypt when Joseph, all his brothers, and the former generation died. In fact with the death of this generation, what the Israelites experienced was a deep loss and symbolic disconnection from God's declared legacy to them. As a result, they did not know their true identity and were treated far less than their worth. The Bible notes that in this experience, they suffered abuse, harsh labour and oppression (Exodus 1:8-14).

God's investment in the Israelites reconnection to His Word did not fail however. He had a plan to restore their identity through Moses' miraculous life. God demonstrated this plan by choosing Moses to be a foundational voice of His Word in the Israelite's deliverance. As with the coming of Jesus Christ, this process of deliverance was really about restoring the original Word of God to this generation.

In the same way, your legacy is about sharing words today that will revive intangible generational blessings as a life line for the next generation. Similar to Moses, the words you pen today will be a deeply meaningful legacy for the future. Your words have power!

Legacy Moments – Your Legacy

About You

Meaningful details, affirming moments, and stories about your child/loved one

Your life has unique details and moments that hold special meaning about who you are. These details and moments are important to know because they help to define you.

Whether it's discovering the meaning of your name, or a beginning story about the details of your birth, the creation of a significant family relationship, a note about your unique qualities, or an affirming story, reminders of these moments and details will touch your life in special ways. As a part of your legacy, they carry the lasting impact of love and affirming connection that will be foundational to your personal identity.

Transferring love, identity and connection to your child or loved one

"A good name is to be chosen rather than great riches..." (Proverbs 22:1)

Your Name:

The Meaning of Your Name or reason You Were Given this Name:

A name defines you...

A name surrounds you...

A name will lead and follow you...

Live to preserve the best name!

"I will make your name great, like the names of the greatest men of the earth." (2 Samuel 7:9)

Meaningful words shape a lasting legacy. "...Declare a thing, and it will be established for you." Job 22:28

A Legacy Letter to You...

You are a blessing and a gift from God (Psalm 127:3)

DATE _____   SIGNED_____

There is something in all of us that makes us wonder about where and how we began. Somehow this story lends much to our sense of worth and identity. The Bible declares that in the beginning, "God saw everything that He had made, and indeed it was very good." Genesis 1:31

Your Beginning Story

A story or note of special moments that uniquely define you (Before you were born, the experience of your birth, adoption process, getting to know you…)

DATE _____   SIGNED_____

"I will praise You, for I am fearfully and wonderfully made; marvellous are Your works, and that my soul knows very well." Psalm 139:14

Your defining qualities

Some special things about you

DATE _____   SIGNED_____

Stories paint pictures as pictures tell stories. "A word fitly spoken is like apples of gold in settings of silver."

Proverbs 25:11

A Picture That Tells A Story

A picture that says a lot about who you are

DATE _____   SIGNED_____

"I will praise You, O LORD, with my whole heart; I will tell of all Your marvellous works." Psalm 9:1

A Meaningful Story/Testimony About You

Life moments (happy/challenging) that are filled with deep meaning, and for which we are thankful

DATE _____   SIGNED_____

"To everything there is a season, [and] a time for every purpose under heaven" You were meant to be in this time! – Ecclesiastes 3:1-7

Important Dates and Details

Birthdays, places of birth, anniversaries, and important information about you or other special people in our family/ life

DATE _____   SIGNED_____

Who You Are:

Other meaningful details, stories, or affirming moments with you

DATE _____   SIGNED_____

Who You Are:

Other meaningful details, stories, or affirming moments with you

DATE _____   SIGNED_____

Who You Are:

Other meaningful details, stories, or affirming moments with you

DATE _____   SIGNED_____

A Family Legacy:

Wisdom and principles from the past

In many cultures today, the young and old remain vastly disconnected. With the passing of time, we have moved further and further away from the wisdom of the past and ultimately from a place of togetherness or unity, where the blessings of God dwell (Psalm 133:1,3b).

The secure days, when elders (adults or parents) and children spent regular times sharing meaningful things with each other, are lost. Today's busy lifestyle, material focus, and prevalence of technology continue to force many families away from what we often refer to as 'quality time' together.

There is a need to restore the strength of intergenerational connections. The wisdom of yesterday needs to be intentionally shared, as it is crucial to the success of tomorrow.

By defining who you are as a parent/parent figure, sharing lessons learned, generational lifelines, principles, blessings and strengths, you will in fact rebuild an intergenerational bridge that would otherwise remain broken. For while the advancement of the current century is rich, the knowledge and wisdom in a parent's legacy will forever remain unquestionably priceless.

Bridging generational gaps by sharing my life story with you and the generations to come.

"Behold, how good and how pleasant it is, for brethren to dwell together in unity!...For there the LORD commanded the blessing - life forevermore." Psalm 133:1,3b

"Gold there is, and rubies in abundance, but lips that speak knowledge are a rare jewel." Proverbs 20:15 (NIV)

A Beginning Story – A Family Legacy

A defining story about 'who I am' including: place of birth, experience growing up, strengths/unique qualities, challenges I've overcome, dreams or achievements

DATE _____   SIGNED_____

Many lessons are learned from what may seem like failures THEN. NOW will always present a new opportunity for a better end. Ecclesiastes 7:8; Hebrews 11:1

Important Lessons Learned

Some valuable things to know from the life journey of your parents/guardians

DATE _____   SIGNED_____

"Show me Your ways, O LORD; Teach me Your paths. Lead me in Your truth and teach me, for You are the God of my salvation." Psalm 25:4-5

Important Things to Know About Your Paternal Extended Family:

Details about background and family

DATE _____   SIGNED_____

"...Blessed be the name of God forever and ever, for wisdom and might are His. And He changes the times and the seasons; He removes kings and raises up kings; He gives wisdom to the wise and knowledge to those who have understanding. He reveals deep and secret things..." Daniel 2:20-22

Important Things to Know About Your Maternal Extended Family:

Details about background and family

DATE _____   SIGNED_____

"The Lord has been mindful of us: He will bless us..." "The Lord shall increase you more and more, you and your children." Psalm 115:12; Psalm 115:14 (KJV)

Our Legacy Lifeline:

Family tree or generational pictures of loved ones or significant people

DATE _____   SIGNED_____

The strength of the past is vital for the future. Indeed "there shall come forth a Rod from the stem of Jesse, and a Branch shall grow out of his roots." For the "...dominion [of God] is from generation to generation." Isaiah 11:1; Daniel 4:3

Our Generational Strengths or Blessings

Specific strengths, talents, gifts/blessings that have been in our family lineage

DATE _____   SIGNED_____

Elders are like the wealth of many nations. Similar to biblical streams of water, the legacy of who they are will always give life to the depth of who you will become. Exodus 18; Leviticus 19:32; Proverbs 17:6; Ezekiel 47:1-9

Principles Learned From Our Elders

Key life principles learned from our elders or impactful achievements they have made

DATE _____   SIGNED_____

Never let the understanding you lack block you from the blessing you need. Strive to grow in holistic understanding.

Proverbs 4:7-8

Cultural Milestones or Struggles

Important things to know about our native and current culture

DATE _____   SIGNED_____

Family Legacy

Other wisdom and principles from the past

DATE _____   SIGNED_____

Family Legacy

Other wisdom and principles from the past

DATE _____   SIGNED_____

Family Legacy

Other wisdom and principles from the past

DATE _____   SIGNED_____

"So he answered and said, You shall love the LORD your God with all your heart, with all your soul, with all your strength, and with all your mind, and your neighbor as yourself." Deuteronomy 6:4-5; Luke 10:27

A Priceless Principle

Some experiences in your life may seem unfair. Yet these same experiences may also hold particular wisdom for your future. They often come our way to help us reflect the heart of God and ultimately draw us to live out his witness in some of the most challenging but meaningful ways.

Throughout the Books of 1 and 2 Samuel (I Samuel 18 - II Samuel 1), we see an intense demonstration of relational tension between Saul and David. Given the fact that Saul consistently sought to take David's life, naturally, one may think that when David was given an open opportunity to retaliate, he would have taken Saul's life. Yet, that was not his response.

When David had an opportunity to experience Saul in a place of vulnerability, he made a decision not to hurt him. He rather embraced a priceless principle by acknowledging that God Himself was the one who anointed Saul as king, and God Himself was still in charge. Retaliation was therefore not an option.

David acknowledged that he had no right to harm Saul or willfully act in a way that would remove him from the office in which God had placed him. In so doing, David demonstrated a heart to manifest God's will even in this moment where circumstances compelled him to do otherwise. As a result, God not only kept David safe during his time as a fugitive, but also caused him to ultimately rise as king.

While David may have faced significant battles throughout his reign, both from without and within, he somehow held on to this principle of turning back unto God with a heart to live in His will.

God's response to David spoke to generations! He made a covenant with David, declaring that not only would he be king, but that there would always be a king amongst his descendants as long as they too continued to maintain the principle of following God's commandments. Jesus, the King of kings, ultimately came from this lineage!

Values:

The core standard of our family or life together

Values are the deep standards by which we live. They can be described as the heartbeat of our lives as they define how we effectively relate with each other.

Important values could include standards like honesty, godliness, family togetherness, excellence, and integrity. Whether passed on from the customs of previous generations, or current in the principles by which you live today, sharing important values will allow their inherent meaning and character building benefit to be successfully transferred to your loved ones across generations.

Each moment of life, when placed together, becomes an indescribable picture
of legacy for the future!

"It takes wisdom to have a good family, and it takes understanding to make it strong. It takes knowledge to fill a home with rare and beautiful treasures." Proverbs 24:3-4

Our Most Important Life Values

These are the everyday and meaningful values that define who we are and how we conduct ourselves

DATE _____   SIGNED_____

Vision is the foundation to future manifestation. For each family, it is the statement that will faithfully remind you of your purpose and legacy. "Where there is no vision, the people perish: but he that keepeth the law, happy is he." Proverbs 29:18 (KJV)

Our Legacy Vision Statement

An easy to remember statement that reminds us of our life goals and values

DATE _____   SIGNED_____

Prayer is communication and communion with God. The psalmist reflected this well, saying, "Show me Your ways, O LORD; Teach me Your paths. Lead me in Your truth and teach me, for You are the God of my salvation..." Psalm 25:4-5

The Values or Legacy of Our Spiritual Faith

What our faith community believes, important spiritual principles/practices we value, and significant achievements we have made

DATE _____   SIGNED_____

Values

Other core standards of our family and life together

DATE _____   SIGNED_____

Values

Other core standards of our family and life together

DATE _____   SIGNED_____

Values

Other core standards of our family and life together

DATE _____   SIGNED_____

Symbols and Visual Representations

Whether new or passed on from previous generations, symbols generally carry deep meaning far beyond their visual presentation. If this meaning remains vague or unknown, the rich value of the symbol is diminished. It may be a family heirloom, a great picture or a piece of art, a symbolic ritual or even a traditional recipe. The important question is: what meaning does this symbol hold and why is it meaningful?

Identifying important symbols and the meaning they carry will promote a profound sense of identity in you and your child or loved one. It will also support the fullest influence of each symbol across generations.

One example of a symbol and its attached generational meaning is recorded in the children of Israel's exodus journey. "Moses said, "This is what the LORD has commanded: 'Take an omer of manna and keep it for the generations to come, so they can see the bread I gave you to eat in the wilderness when I brought you out of Egypt.'" (Exodus 16:32 NIV). The symbolism contained in this manna was much more than the obvious. For generations to come, it would be a rich representation of God's supernatural provision.

Communicate important meaning through symbols, pictures, and art that reflect generational value for you and your child or loved one.

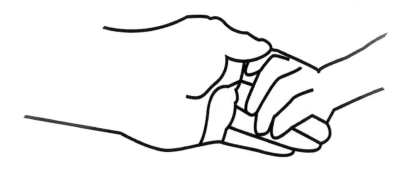

A Generational Picture of Meaning and Identity

"He told them another parable: "The kingdom of heaven is like a mustard seed, which a man took and planted in his field. Though it is the smallest of all seeds, yet when it grows, it is the largest of garden plants and becomes a tree, so that the birds come and perch in its branches."

Mathew 13:31-32 (NIV)

Like the olive branch, a symbol is much more than just an emblem. It is a meaningful reminder of great moments now and great promises to come. Genesis 8:11

A Symbol That Describes You

A symbol that says a lot about you (may include personal expressive art)

DATE _____   SIGNED_____

Who you are will be known by the symbolic marks that define you. Exodus 12:13; Revelation 7:2-3

Our Symbolic Imprint

A family crest or symbol that best defines the strength and identity of our relationship

DATE _____   SIGNED_____

"And Moses built an altar and called its name, The-LORD-Is-My-Banner; for he said, because the LORD has sworn: the LORD will have war with Amalek [the enemy] from generation to generation." Exodus 17:15-16

Spiritual Symbols

Important spiritual symbols and their meaning (may include the cross, the altar, etc.)

DATE _____   SIGNED_____

"Lord, you have been our dwelling place throughout all generations. Before the mountains were born or you brought forth the whole world, from everlasting to everlasting you are God." Psalm 90:1-2 (NIV)

Symbolic Traditions

Meaningful rituals, traditions, cultural celebrations or ceremonies that we practice regularly or on special occasions, and their meaning to us

DATE _____   SIGNED_____

As bread is a symbol of the body of Christ in the Bible, different foods have held cultural symbolic meaning for many generations. John 6:48; 1 Corinthians 11:23-26

Symbolic Food

A special/traditional recipe or type of food that is symbolically meaningful to us and why

DATE _____   SIGNED_____

"I urge, then, first of all, that petitions, prayers, intercession and thanksgiving be made for all people— for kings and all those in authority, that we may live peaceful and quiet lives in all godliness and holiness. This is good, and pleases God our Savior," 1Timothy 2:1-3(NIV)

National Symbols

National or geographic symbols that hold great meaning, including the national flag, anthem, historic places, national leaders/role models, and their symbolic meaning

DATE _____   SIGNED_____

Symbols

Other symbolic information and meaning

DATE _____   SIGNED_____

Symbols

Other symbolic information and meaning

DATE _____   SIGNED_____

Symbols

Other symbolic information and meaning

DATE _____   SIGNED_____

Life Instructions: A Roadmap For The Future

Any road that is paved with effective instructions will lend to a most productive journey. As I have walked through different stages of my own life, "don't reinvent the wheel" is a statement that has truly been a shrewd reminder that "What has been will be again, what has been done will be done again; there is nothing new under the sun." Ecclesiastes 1:9 (NIV).

In every generation, God has intentionally echoed His voice through someone, so that His covenant instructions for godliness and success will be known. Indeed, "All Scripture is given by inspiration of God, and is profitable for doctrine, for reproof, for correction, for instruction in righteousness" (2 Timothy 3:16). Through meaningful instructions, each generation is given the opportunity to avoid the mistakes of the past and rather forge ahead into the future with precision.

Instructing the next generation about key life matters will no doubt serve to minimize the mistakes of the past while supporting a future reality of 'right paths' for God's glory. (Psalm 23:3; Proverbs 4:11)

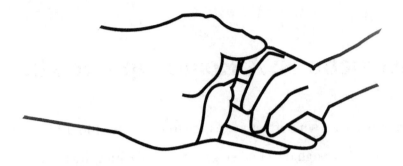

"Apply your heart to instruction, and your ears to words of knowledge. Never pay back evil with more evil. Do things in such a way that everyone can see you are honourable." For "This is what the LORD says - your Redeemer, the Holy One of Israel: "I am the LORD your God, who teaches you what is best for you, who directs you in the way you should go." Proverbs 23:12; Romans 12:17 (NLT); Isaiah 48:17 (NIV)

"For God so loved the world that He gave His only begotten Son, that whoever believes in Him should not perish but have everlasting life. For God did not send His Son into the world to condemn the world, but that the world through Him might be saved." John 3:16-17

About Practically Living Your Faith

Instructions on a personal relationship with Jesus Christ

DATE _____   SIGNED_____

"Because you have loved good and hated wrong; God has set you above your companions by anointing you with the oil of joy." Psalm 45:7; Hebrews 1:9

About Sound Judgment and Character

Instructions on upholding integrity even when faced with tough decisions

DATE _____   SIGNED_____

There are some people in your life who are definitely God-sent. They may sometimes be a source of pain, yet treat them with humility and honour. As with Ruth and Naomi, the unfolding of your legacy may be intricately tied to them. Ruth 1:14-18

About Friendships/Relationships

Instructions on choosing and being a good friend

DATE _____   SIGNED_____

"And now abide faith, hope, love, these three; but the greatest of these is love."

1 Corinthians 13:13

About Love and Marriage

Instructions on preparing for and embracing this gift

DATE _____   SIGNED_____

"...Good people who live honest lives will be a blessing to their children." Proverbs 20:7 (NCV)

About Parenting

Instructions on caring for anyone placed in your care

DATE _____   SIGNED_____

"The rich rules over the poor, and the borrower is servant to the lender. He who has a generous eye will be blessed, for he gives of his bread to the poor." Proverbs 22:7,9

About Finances

Instructions on managing money and the importance of debt freedom

DATE _____   SIGNED_____

"Being confident of this very thing, that He who has begun a good work in you will complete it until the day of Jesus Christ"; "Therefore do not cast away your confidence, which has great reward." Philippians 1:6; Hebrews 10:3

About Confidence and Endurance

Believing in who you are and seeing yourself as God sees you

DATE _____   SIGNED_____

Life Instruction

Other important life instructions

DATE _____   SIGNED_____

Life Instruction

Other important life instructions

DATE _____   SIGNED _____

Life Instruction

Other important life instructions

DATE _____   SIGNED_____

Legacy Declarations/Decrees and Prophetic Blessings

I have heard many testimonies throughout my lifetime, but one of the most common goes like this: 'I was lost, but the prayers of my mother brought me back.' When I think about the power of decrees/declarations, I think about this type of testimony.

The words 'decree' and 'declaration' are often used interchangeably and point to how we can actively employ the word of God to prophesy or compel destined change in our lives. This reality is rooted in the knowledge of God's Word, boldness in believing it, speaking it, and then seeing it come to pass. The Bible says it this way, "You will also declare a thing, and it will be established for you" (Job 22:28).

As you make decrees, believe that you are indeed prophesying and bringing God in remembrance of His promises through His Word (Isaiah 43:26). As you faithfully declare the will of God about your child or loved one, God has promised to be faithful to the faithful (Psalm 101:6); to acknowledge the declaration of his Word for the generations to come (Isaiah 55:11); and to faithfully remember His generational covenant towards you and your children's children (Exodus 2:24-25).

Include declarations/decrees and prophetic blessings about your child or loved one's

purpose and destiny

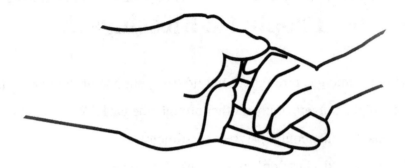

"And I will give you the keys of the kingdom of heaven, and whatever you bind on earth will be bound in heaven, and whatever you loose on earth will be loosed in heaven." Matthew 16:19

<u>A Decree</u>

The presence of God will reign in every moment of your life. The wisdom of God will activate His rich promises for your entire life. Like an arrow in the hand of a warrior, you are sharp and disciplined. You shall be taught by the Lord Himself and great shall be your peace as you love Him. In key decisions, God Himself will pour out His Spirit upon you. In life, you will run to Him and He will guard you. You will always be the head; never the tail. You will excel in all you put your hands to do, and in God you will never fail.

You are shielded from every worldly pressure and will always know your divine worth.

You are destined to be a pillar of strength, honour, and integrity in this world. You will forever be protected as a special treasure. You are blessed to be a lender; never a borrower; a leader; never a follower. You are a true gift from God and a crowning glory to your family!

I speak into you an inheritance of godly living in every day to come, a life rooted in faith, and the fullness of God at the heart of every moment you live.

You are blessed!

"And all the days of my life were written in Your book before any of them came to be". I have a unique place and purpose in the world. Psalm 139:16 and cf. Psalm 139:14; Ephesians 2:10

A Declaration About Your Unique Purpose

Purposeful gifts and talents in you

DATE _____   SIGNED_____

"The Lord GOD has given me the tongue of the learned, that I should know how to speak a word in season to him who is weary. He awakens me morning by morning, He awakens my ear to hear as the learned." Isaiah 50:4

A Prophetic Blessing for Your Future

A declaration for lifelong manifestation of your very best

DATE _____   SIGNED_____

"You shall be blessed above all peoples. There shall not be male or female barren among you..." For "...you are a chosen generation [and] a royal priesthood, a holy nation, His own special people, that you may proclaim the praises of Him who called you out of darkness into His marvellous light." Deuteronomy 7:14; 1 Peter 2:9

A Blessing for Your Generational Success

A blessing given to you and your children's children

DATE _____   SIGNED_____

A Blessing/Decree/Declaration/Prophecy

Other important blessings/decrees/declarations/prophecies

DATE _____   SIGNED_____

A Blessing/Decree/Declaration/Prophecy

Other important blessings/decrees/declarations/prophecies

DATE _____   SIGNED_____

A Blessing/Decree/Declaration/Prophecy

Other important blessings/decrees/declarations/prophecies

DATE _____   SIGNED_____

Your Own Legacy Moments Title Pages

There may be important elements that are unique to your relationship and legacy that may not have been captured in the preceding sections of *Legacy Moments*. The following pages will allow you to create your own titles and the opportunity to share these special pages of your legacy.

"...the LORD your God is God; He is the faithful God, keeping his covenant of love to a thousand generations of those who love him and keep his commandments."

Deuteronomy 7:9

DATE _____   SIGNED_____

DATE _____   SIGNED_____

DATE _____   SIGNED_____

DATE _____   SIGNED_____

DATE _____   SIGNED_____

DATE _____   SIGNED_____

DATE _____   SIGNED_____

DATE _____   SIGNED_____

DATE _____   SIGNED_____

DATE _____   SIGNED_____

"Now to Him who is able to do exceeding abundantly above all that we ask or think, according to the power that works in us, to Him *be* glory in the church by Christ Jesus to all generations, forever and ever. Amen!"
Ephesians 3:20-21

CPSIA information can be obtained
at www.ICGtesting.com
Printed in the USA
BVHW011311060621
608890BV00012B/796